THE OFFICIAL
Wolves
ANNUAL 2012

Written by Paul Berry

Designed by Cavan Convery

A Grange Publication

ISBN: 978-1-908221-40-7

£7.9

Contents

MICK McCARTHY
an exclusive club

Heading into his third season in charge of Wolves in the Barclays Premier League has taken Mick McCarthy into a pretty exclusive club when it comes to Molineux managers.

By our reckoning, only five occupants of the Wolverhampton Wanderers hotseat have presided over a longer spell in the country's top division.

There is some conjecture over whether Jack Addenbrooke or a committee was in charge of Wolves in their early years – or indeed a combination of both – when they chalked up 18 years in the top division.

The legendary Stan Cullis enjoyed 16 seasons in charge of Wolves in the top flight, Bill McGarry approximately eight and Major Frank Buckley seven prior to World War Two.

The only post-war manager to nudge out McCarthy is John Barnwell, who spent three years and two months in the old Division One from 1978-82.

The boss is also one of just three, alongside Buckley and Sammy Chung, to achieve promotion to the top flight as champions, and of the six who have taken Wolves into the top division, is only surpassed by Buckley in terms of subsequent experience.

The current Wolves manager is however not one to spend too much time checking out statistics or indeed wallowing in any personal glory.

But the figures above are particularly impressive given the massive disparity between the big clubs and the rest since the advent of the Barclays Premier League almost 20 years ago.

McCarthy also headed into the current campaign standing at number eight in terms of the longest serving managers in the four English divisions. More evidence if it were needed of the success of the job undertaken at Molineux.

A third successive Premier League season is progress indeed from the day McCarthy first walked into the Compton training ground on July 24, 2006.

He was met by a depleted and morale-sapped squad affected by the loss of the parachute payments following relegation, but quickly set about relaunching the good ship Wolves to hugely positive effect.

As mentioned, he doesn't go in for much personal reflection, or living in the past, but will accept a degree of delight in the progress made at all levels during his five years at the helm.

"Matt Murray was injured but came in later, so it was Oakes in goal," Mick says of the first friendly of his reign.

Edwards, Clyde, Craddock, McNamara, Ricketts, Olofinjana, O'Connor, Rosa, Cort, Clarke – and I think Frankowski was one of the subs.

"I think Lee Naylor and Mark Davies were injured for that game, but that was pretty much all we had.

There was a £1million transfer budget and £1.5million to pay wages.

"So from there we signed Breeny (Gary Breen), Karl Henry, Jay Bothroyd, Craig Davies and Jemal Johnson.

It doesn't make any odds for me looking back – I've just got all sorts in a book from then and stuff from Ireland and just find it interesting to look at.

It's been five years now – I don't look any older do I?

I remember I was in Portugal having lost my job at Sunderland and was thinking hopefully I'd get a chance at another one.

If I remember right Derby came up, Sheffield United, Leeds – and all went without so much as a call!

Then I got the call from Jez and I think it's turned out to be a good call for all of us."

The boss is not prone to championing his own achievements, but it is difficult to hide a sense of satisfaction at how far the club has come in those five years in registering a feat not seen for three decades.

Equally however, much of the praise is deflected towards the players and backroom staff who have played a major part in the club's progress.

"It's not for me to talk anything up but I am pleased with my five years work," said the boss.

"I can't help but be happy with the five years of graft.

But I've been ably assisted by Taff (Ian Evans) and Dave (Bowman) and then by Terry and Dave.

And we've got a great back-up team with Dales (Tony Daley), Steve Weaver, Pat Mountain, Kempy (Steve Kemp)

and the medical team – everyone in fact.

I could go through them all.

But I am not content though – I want to be better next year, just like everyone else."

Much of the credit is also passed by the manager to the group of players he has assembled, who have – like the club – progressed significantly in recent years.

Many of those signed by McCarthy have been on an upwardly mobile curve which has continued to rise after arriving at Molineux.

And while there is an old saying about familiarity breeding contempt, it is quite the opposite at Wolves, where the team spirit, togetherness and indeed success – keeps the tight knit unit compact.

"We've been very lucky - and smart and clever – with players that we have signed," adds the boss.

"They have fitted into the ethos of the club and they have been prepared to put a shift in, and have been hard-working, diligent and great lads.

I never hear anybody talking about our club and players in disparaging terms like they do about some other Premier League clubs and players.

Not all signings have been good signings, and some haven't worked out, but that's just the way it is and part of the rich tapestry that is a football club.

I have been here five years and a lot of the players have been with me for most of that time.

So of course motivation always becomes an issue, with the players hearing the same things in training and team talks.

But when you're successful it always helps, and there's Terry (Connor) as well and the other coaches – it's not just my voice all the time.

And if your methods work people will trust what you say and believe you."

It's that level of belief and togetherness which McCarthy hopes will once again lead to a successful season in 2011/12. And in doing so, continue to extend his Molineux top flight tenure even further.

ALL WE NEED IS...

There was certainly an element of 'try before you buy' with Wolves' purchase of midfielder Jamie O'Hara.

But Wolves were certainly very quick to make their mind up over a move for the Dartford-born 25-year-old once he swiftly settled in to life at Molineux.

O'Hara's arrival on loan from Tottenham in January came with an option to make the deal permanent in the summer should all parties agree.

The man himself spoke very positively about that prospect right from the very start, an opinion shared by boss Mick McCarthy who quickly spotted his value to the team.

"He also built up a good rapport with the fans," said McCarthy.

"Scoring a really good goal against West Brom was always going to help in that respect!"

Indeed it did.

One swing of the trusty O'Hara left boot at The Hawthorns added to his unquestionable early promise, and set the tone for an impressive overall contribution which led to him becoming the first permanent arrival of the summer, putting pen to paper on a five-year contract.

It was a deal he couldn't wait to get done.

"The club has been a different class ever since I joined," said O'Hara.

"From the moment I walked in here everyone has been brilliant.

I was delighted to get it all done,

and as soon as the season finished, it was a case of getting pen to paper.

It was just about getting it done, and to sign a five-year deal, I couldn't ask for more.

It was the first time since I was 17 and joined Tottenham that I'd signed a long-term deal.

This is the first time I'm going into a club where I don't need to catch up or meet new people.

My family have settled well in the area and we all really enjoyed it from the start."

That rapport from the fans certainly played a major part in O'Hara being keen to commit his long term future to a new life in the Midlands.

His never-say-die attitude, coupled with his undoubted quality, and of course THAT goal, ensured the player-supporter relationship got off to an excellent start.

"I think the goal at The Hawthorns helped!" he admits when reflecting on what turned out to be Wolves' Goal of the Season.

"I didn't even realise it was a big local derby until I joined here.

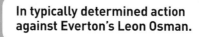

In typically determined action against Everton's Leon Osman.

Then when I scored in it, the reaction and praise I got afterwards made me realise how big the club was and how big a following it has got.

Now I know how big some of these games are.

And if I can really get the fans on my side and put in the performances for the manager, then it's going to be something special to be involved in.

I'm one of those players who wears his heart on his sleeve.

If I'm disappointed you can tell and if I'm overjoyed you can tell.

That's how I've always played – I give 110 per cent.

I want to make the fans happy, and that's the type of player I am.

Hopefully this season we can really push on as a club and I can be a big part of that."

It is that five year contract which is set to play a key part in O'Hara's career development, given his chances at Tottenham were limited, prompting several loan spells, notably at Portsmouth, where he cleaned up in Pompey's Player of the Year awards despite their relegation.

The security of such a long term deal means not only can O'Hara lay down some more permanent roots off the pitch, but also aim to cement his status as a Premier League regular on it as well.

"I wouldn't have signed for five years unless I wanted to be here for five years," he says.

It's going to take me up until I'm 30, and I see my future being here.

I've always said I wanted to be at a club for a long period of time and play 300-400 games for a club. That's what I'm looking to do here.

It was painful to leave because I always wanted to play for Tottenham.

I played over 50 games for them and I was part of the club for a long period of time.

I've always supported them and I still love the club

Sharing a joke with Matt Jarvis.

– it's a fantastic club.

But now I'm a Wolves fan and a Wolves player.

It's time to move on and play 300-400 games for this club."

O'Hara arrived permanently this summer at an exciting time for Wolves.

Not only were a group of determined players fully focused on continuing the club's improvement of recent years, but with the launch of the redevelopment of Molineux there are certainly promising times ahead.

"I think once the stadium is complete here, we'll start filling it and it's going to be fantastic to play here," said O'Hara.

I always love playing home games here, hopefully I can do it every week and start getting some big games under my belt because I think there's more to come from me.

It's our third season in the Premier League, but if you stand still, that's when you're going to come unstuck.

I think this season we've got to push on as a club and as a team, and we can do that.

The first season in the Premier League is about not being pushed over by anyone, then the second season is about doing a little bit more, and in that third season you need to become an established Premier League side and that's what we can do this year.

End of season celebration time with partner Danielle and son Archie.

I think this group of players have something about them.

At all the clubs I've been at, I've never been involved with a group of lads like this.

We're all so close-knit, which shows how close the club is and I think that's why we stayed up – because of the character of the players.

We stuck together and we got the points we needed when everyone had written us off.

I think that's something special to be involved in."

This is one player in particular who's keen to live up to his terrace chant and prove – as the song goes – that "all we need is" indeed Jamie O'Hara.

SEASON REVIEW 2010/11

August

Could Wolves build from their first ever survival in the Barclays Premier League and go on to improve on a more than decent 15th position in 2009/10?

Or would they fall victim – like so many before them – to the dreaded 'second season syndrome' as they set out after a mixed pre-season of results which included a successful week in Ireland?

Stoke at Molineux on the opening day served up an interesting barometer given that the Potters were 12 months down the line on Wolves in terms of Premier League experience.

But, despite missing the influential Kevin Doyle with injury, it was his joint record signing partner-in-crime Steven Fletcher whose close range debut goal ultimately proved the difference between the two sides in Wolves' 2-1 win.

Fletcher's effort however was overshadowed in terms of quality by a superbly executed free kick from David Jones, who took a tapped lay-off from Karl Henry, flicked the ball up and volleyed past Thomas Sorensen to get Molineux's new season off to a scintillating start.

Buoyed by the first opening day win in some 11 years, Wolves travelled to Everton and hit back from being over-run in the first half to equalise through Sylvan Ebanks-Blake and almost snatch all three points late on.

After edging out Southend in the Carling Cup – Richard Stearman providing the winner in the last seconds of injury time of extra time – Wolves welcomed Newcastle on the last weekend of the month knowing victory could put them right to the top end of the embryonic league table.

What followed was 90 minutes of pure footballing theatre in a throwback to blood-and-thunder battles of old, with no quarter asked or given from either team.

Wolves may have been highlighted in the evening's Match of the Day package for a so-called targeting of Joey Barton, but in reality both sides gave as good as they got in a hugely entertaining 90 minutes.

The game? Oh yes. It finished 1-1, with Ebanks-Blake's superb opener for Wolves cancelled out by a towering header from the in-form and Liverpool-destined Andy Carroll.

August was also the month which saw the sad news of the retirement of popular Wolves keeper Matt Murray, finally forced to hang up his gloves after a long-running battle with injury.

September

A decent first month of the season in which a win and two draws saw Wolves occupying a lofty fourth position in the Barclays Premier League looked even better at half time at Craven Cottage, as Jelle Van Damme's first goal for the club put Wolves in front.

But Fulham's Moussa Dembele restored parity shortly after half time, and, after Christophe Berra's late dismissal, fired a free kick through the wall to deny Wolves even a point.

In the wake of the hype following the hard-fought Toon tussle seven days earlier, the normally mild-mannered Fulham supporters directed some pretty strong stuff at Wolves' team and management, not least as Karl Henry's legitimate and ball winning tackle on Bobby Zamora unfortunately left the England striker with a broken leg after he fell awkwardly.

Wolves were back in London at Tottenham a week later, Henry receiving a rapturous reception from the travelling fans in defiance of having become something of a media whipping boy, but once again the team found themselves pegged back after taking the lead.

Steven Fletcher had broken the deadlock with a predatory close-range finish right on half time, but Wolves were denied a second successive White Hart Lane surprise by three Spurs goals in the final 13 minutes.

Wolves did return to winning ways in the next round of the Carling Cup, albeit with another struggle as substitute strikers Kevin Doyle (2) and Fletcher helped secure a 4-2 extra time victory against Notts County.

But the return to league action brought more misery due to a late sucker punch, as Aston Villa's Emile Heskey powered home an excellent late header after Matt Jarvis had snuffed out Stewart Downing's opener.

Following Zamora's unfortunate injury for Fulham it was bad news for Adlene Guedioura, who suffered a similar fate after a challenge from Villa substitute Steve Sidwell.

October

A busy old month was October, and one which finished a lot better than it started.

With both sides already occupying two of the bottom four spots in the Barclays Premier League table, a trip to the DW Stadium to face Wigan carried all the hallmarks of an early season six-pointer.

But the loss of Karl Henry to a red card following an 11th minute challenge on Jordi Gomez left Wolves with an uphill battle, albeit one which they handled well until the same Wigan player lashed home a free kick after the hour mark.

Hugo Rodallega sealed Wigan's 2-0 win, and Wolves were unable to completely bounce back against another team of early strugglers when West Ham visited Molineux seven days later.

Matt Jarvis's well-executed 10th minute finish put Wolves a goal to the good, but Mark Noble earned the Hammers a point with a coolly-taken penalty shortly after the interval.

The draw left Wolves second bottom in the table ahead of a daunting sequence of fixtures, the first of which was champions Chelsea at Stamford Bridge.

Yet a 2-0 defeat and eighth successive league game without victory did not tell the full story, as Wolves peppered Petr Cech's goal with no fewer than nine shots on target and were right in the game until Salomon Kalou's 81st minute clincher.

It was an impressive level of performance, which Wolves then

repeated in the Carling Cup at Manchester United, George Elokobi and Kevin Foley twice equalising before Javier Hernandez's last gasp winner put the Red Devils through.

Confidence was rising however, and a third successive meeting with one of the Premier League 'big boys' – Manchester City - finally produced a deserved success.

Wolves had to come from behind to do it after Emmanuel Adebayor's early penalty, but Nenad Milijaš quickly levelled and Dave Edwards popped up with a priceless second three minutes before the hour mark.

After several near misses, Wolves had finally landed a major Premier League scalp and, not for the last time in the season, had proved they had the character to tough it out when the chips were down.

November

So after beating one half of Manchester it was off to face the others – and this time on their own patch.

And having seen off City at Molineux , Wolves went agonisingly and indeed painfully close to picking up a draw at United.

Sylvan Ebanks-Blake's equaliser at his former club looked for all the world as if it would earn undaunted Wolves another priceless point, but with seconds of injury time remaining United did what United do so often, as Ji-Sung Park's low shot beat Marcus Hahnemann.

It was a cruel, cruel blow and one which left the team and manager utterly devastated, having more than matched the Reds over the rest of the game.

Wolves weren't able to run Arsenal as close next time out at Molineux, but they weren't far off.

Behind after just 38 seconds to Marouane Chamakh, Wolves did get close to an equaliser particularly, through Christophe Berra late on, but after Lukasz Fabianski's fine save the action switched to the other end for Chamakh to get his second.

The late goals had turned into early goals and, an unfortunate Richard Stearman own goal just 46 seconds into the game with Bolton proved the precursor to conceding two more after the hour.

Kevin Foley and Steven Fletcher did rally by finding the net, but it was too little too late as Bolton ran out 3-2 winners.

By the time Wolves went down 2-1 at Blackpool with Kevin Doyle's header nothing more than a consolation, they had lost four league games in succession and won just one in 13.

Then, five points adrift of the safety zone, they were also 2-1 adrift against Sunderland with ten minutes remaining, before Stephen Hunt dragged the team level.

And when Ebanks-Blake controlled and fired home in the final minute of normal time, the celebrations of the entire Wolves bench proved just how vital the famous win could prove.

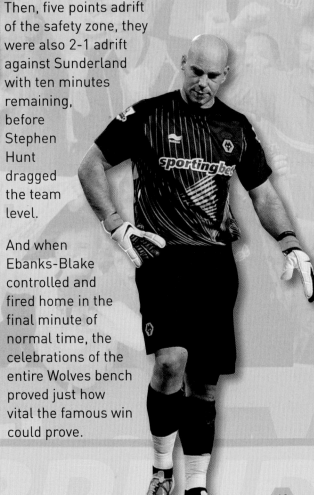

December

December was another month of ups and downs for all things Wolves.

After the high of the last minute win against Sunderland in November came the low of another disappointing performance at Blackburn, as Wolves crashed to a 3-0 defeat.

Having said that, Stephen Ward and Ronald Zubar both fired against the woodwork before Blackburn's opening goal, and Rovers' keeper Paul Robinson finished up as Man of the Match which, said a lot about the manner of Wolves' performance.

And the positives of that performance were carried into the next home game with Birmingham where, despite being decimated by injury, Wolves dug deep to register a 1-0 win.

Such was the injury crisis that five of Wolves' seven subs boasted just one Barclays Premier League start between them, but it was a day for big hearts as Stephen Hunt produced a neat first half finish to Sylvan Ebanks-Blake's impressive cross to clinch the points.

Yet the rollercoaster ride continued courtesy of a Boxing Day clash at home to Wigan, when victory could well have taken Wolves out of the bottom three.

What followed however was defeat, a third successive defeat at the hands of the Latics, as Steven Fletcher's late consolation proved meaningless after an early Wigan brace.

But it was very much a case of saving the best till last as far as December was concerned, with a belated Christmas present for the Wolves arriving – with bells on – at Anfield.

Wolves hadn't beaten Liverpool at Anfield in 27 years, but for Steve Mardenborough read Stephen Ward as the versatile Irishman's clinical second half finish proved enough to cap a thoroughly deserved victory.

The crucially-timed success saw Wolves heading into 2011 second from bottom of the table, but only a point adrift of the safety zone.

January

It was a busy January with no fewer than seven fixtures which saw Wolves enter – and exit – the FA Cup.

Nenad Milijaš was heavily involved in the cup action, rifling home a superb 30-yarder in the third round 2-2 draw with Doncaster – after which Wolves won the replay 5-0 – but then missing a last gasp penalty in the fourth round tie with Stoke.

That enabled the Potters to make progress thanks to Robert Huth's header, progress which took them all the way to a Wembley final defeat at the hands of Manchester City.

In the league, the contrasting ups-and-downs continued apace, with the year beginning with a disappointing 2-0 defeat at West Ham which nudged Wolves back to the bottom of the pile.

Yet four days later came another superb and memorable response from Molineux's embattled troops.

Wednesdays were proving particularly profitable for Mick McCarthy's men, and seven days on from the Anfield heroics it was champions Chelsea who were put to the sword at Molineux thanks to Jose Bosingwa diverting Stephen Hunt's early corner into his own net.

Wolves couldn't quite produce a repeat performance at the City of Manchester Stadium next time out in the league, although they did worry the big-spending blue half of Manchester, hitting back from 4-1 down to eventually lose 4-3.

The previous win against Chelsea had actually lifted Wolves out of the bottom three, but they finished the month second from bottom after finding Liverpool under Kenny

Dalglish a far tougher proposition than the December model.

Goals from Raul Meireles and Fernando Torres (2) – his last for Liverpool before moving to Chelsea – were enough to see Wolves off on an afternoon later overshadowed by off-camera comments from Sky's Richard Keys and Andy Gray relating to female assistant referee Sian Massey.

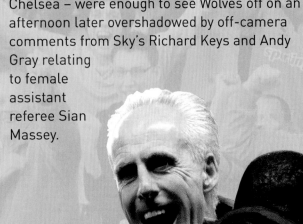

February

If ever there were four days which encapsulated Wolves' Barclays Premier League season then step forward the start of February.

From agony to ecstasy, despair to delight, the trip to Bolton and visit of Manchester United provided a polar extreme of emotions as the dramatic season rumbled on.

At the Reebok Stadium, Wolves, backed by an excellent performance from keeper Wayne Hennessey, went into injury time nursing a very hard-fought and well-earned point.

Then Ronald Zubar failed to look up before passing back to Hennessey, allowing Daniel Sturridge to nip in for the hammerest of hammer blows to leave dressing room and travelling fans utterly despondent.

All of that meant that when Wolves, Zubar and all after a public vote of confidence

from Mick McCarthy, welcomed the unbeaten league leaders to Molineux four days later, they did so from a position once more propping up the rest of the Premier League.

Conceding an early goal to Nani was therefore far from helpful.

But Billy Ocean must have been on the pre-match iPods again – "When the going gets tough the tough get going" – and Wolves hit back with goals from George Elokobi and Kevin Doyle, securing a famous 2-1 win to end United's 29-games unbeaten league run.

Scintillating stuff, and once again proof if ever it were needed of the never-say-die attitude within the Molineux ranks.

A 2-0 defeat to in-form Arsenal followed, before the first ever Premier League Black Country Derby at the Hawthorns, re-arranged after falling victim to the weather in December.

Jamie O'Hara's superb first goal in Wolves colours took the team within sight of another crucial three points, only for Carlos Vela to latch onto a Hennessey parry in injury time to once again dent the survival bid.

Wolves finished the month with their biggest win of the season, hauling Blackpool into the relegation shake-up at the same time with a comfortable 4-0 win, including two from substitute Sylvan Ebanks-Blake.

February was also the month in which Chairman Steve Morgan pressed the button on the Stadium Redevelopment, announcing the exciting news that work on the Stan Cullis Stand would commence at the end of the season.

March

Wolves' first game in March was preceded by an emotional tribute to former defender Dean Richards, who had passed away at the age of 36 after a long and courageous battle with illness.

The fixture computer had thrown up Wolves against another of his former clubs – Tottenham – and representatives from both – Matt Murray and Ledley King – were joined by Bradford chairman Mark Lawn and former Southampton defender Claus Lundevkam in the pitchside tribute.

Richards' widow Samantha and their two sons Rio and Jaden showed extraordinary courage to take part with others present, including Dave Jones, James Beattie, Hassan Kachloul, Graham Taylor and Don Goodman.

If ever there was a fitting tribute to Richards' sad passing, it arrived in the form of the match, a pulsating 90 minutes which – also fittingly – finished up as a draw.

The pendulum switched from side to side, but it was Steven Fletcher's late header from a pinpoint Matt Jarvis cross which earned Wolves a share of the spoils after a six goal thriller.

The FA Cup and an international break made it a strange month in March, with only two matches played.

And the second proved a momentous one for all of a Wolves persuasion by virtue of their first win over Aston Villa in 31 years.

Jarvis was again a key figure, firing home the only goal of the game with an excellent 38th minute volley.

To cap a perfect weekend, the winger then landed his first senior England call-up little over 24 hours later.

When stepping out as a Wembley substitute against Ghana, Jarvis became Wolves' first fully fledged international since Steve Bull over 20 years previously.

April

If the win against Aston Villa had propelled Wolves into a decent position to maintain their long-running survival bid, then April was the month when it suddenly became a far more difficult proposition.

Just one point from four games set the tone for a worrying loss of form at just the time when they needed that form most.

Wolves hadn't been helped by one of many untimely injuries to have afflicted their season when Kevin Doyle damaged his medial knee ligaments whilst on international duty with the Republic of Ireland.

Doyle had once again proved a key performer in Wolves' season, and his partnership with attacking midfielder Jamie O'Hara was reaping particular dividends from the 4-3-3/4-5-1 formation.

The trip to face Newcastle at St James's Park was dominated by pre-match hype suggesting there would be more fireworks in the manner of the no-holds-barred clash at Molineux.

Nothing could have been further from the truth as Wolves found themselves 3-0 down just after half time, a mini-comeback providing little consolation as they were eventually undone 4-1.

The goals also flooded in at the wrong end at home to Everton next time out, three of them thumping into the Wolves net before half time, no further score ensuring the game finished 3-0.

After another two week break due to Stoke's participation in the FA Cup semi finals, Fulham were next up at Molineux, and while it needed a late Andy Johnson goal to cancel out Steven Fletcher's opener, in truth the Cottagers possibly deserved more from an impressive overall performance.

When the rearranged trip up the M6 to Stoke finished in a hugely disappointing 3-0 defeat, Wolves found themselves locked fairly and squarely in the bottom three and needing a major reversal in fortunes if they were to survive.

Could they come out fighting?

May

So May arrived, and it was very much a time of Cometh the hour, cometh the men that are required as Wolves embarked on the final four games which would make or break their Barclays Premier League fate.

First up was a difficult-looking Midlands derby at Carling Cup winners Birmingham, themselves in dire need of points to escape the foot of the table.

In Kevin Doyle's absence and with Sylvan Ebanks-Blake affected by injury, the two 'Steves' of Ward and Fletcher had launched a promising forward partnership, and Ward won an early penalty effortlessly converted by Fletcher to give Wolves the lead.

Seb Larsson equalised, and Blues' midfielder Craig Gardner was then sent off, but the hosts embarked on Operation Draw and denied Wolves the time and space to press home their numerical advantage.

Mick McCarthy was unmoved – "it could be the point that keeps us up" – was his philosophy. How little did he realise how prophetic those words would be!

An even bigger derby came next with West Bromwich Albion, now safe after an excellent run, at Molineux.

Never an afternoon for the faint-hearted, the stakes were even higher for Wolves, but on what can genuinely be called a 'Super Sunday' they swept their rivals aside in the opening 50 minutes. Goals from the in-form Fletcher (2) and Adlene Guedioura paving the way for a crucial 3-1 win.

Wolves were now out of the bottom three, but their rivals were also picking up, and an impressive 3-1 win at Sunderland, including Fletcher again on target, was made even more important by victories for Wigan and Blackpool elsewhere.

It did however take Wolves into the final day at home to Blackburn with their fate in their own hands - but what an afternoon it proved to be.

Trailing 3-0 at half time, Wolves were becoming reliant on other results, but after Jamie O'Hara pulled one back, Stephen Hunt's second proved crucial in forcing Birmingham onto the front foot at Tottenham, ultimately to fruitless effect.

If Wolves could be considered fortunate on that crazy final afternoon, it was fortune which had been in short supply over the previous 37 games, and as such was thoroughly deserved following a remarkable season.

Manchesters United and City, Chelsea and Liverpool were all beaten as Wolves improved on their points tally with 40 and genuinely improved in their football as well.

Survival. Mission accomplished. Molineux began the party of all parties to celebrate securing another top flight season.

DESERT ISLAND CHAIRMAN!

Life as Chairman and owner of Wolverhampton Wanderers, plus all of his other business interests, means that Steve Morgan very rarely gets the chance to pause for thought!

What then would happen if he was dispatched to a desert island for a spell, without any creature comforts or possessions?

What would he take if granted certain wishes? In terms of either actual items or thoughts or memories?

Here is a variation on Desert Island Discs – Steve Morgan style.

WHAT BOOK WOULD YOU TAKE?

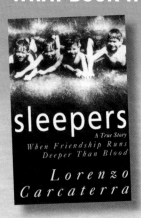

It would be 'Sleepers' by Lorenzo Carcaterra. That's my favourite. I started reading it on holiday one day and I was so wrapped up in it that I couldn't go out for dinner! I finished the book at 2 o'clock in the morning.

WHAT FILM?

My favourite all-time film is 'Four Weddings and a Funeral'. It never fails to cheer me up.

PERSONAL POSSESSION?

Fifteen years ago I was lucky enough to purchase Prince Charles's Aston Martin. It was his personal car which he'd owned for eight years, and there are many pictures of him at polo matches with Princess Di. I take it out only when the sun is shining in the summer months; it's my pride and joy.

WHICH DVD OF A FOOTBALL MATCH WOULD YOU TAKE?

I have so many, but I love watching the highlights of the Wolves home game with Manchester United last season. After going 1-0 down we won 2-1 and played brilliantly throughout. I still haven't made my mind up who scored that second goal – Big George or Doyler?!

PIECE OF MUSIC?

I like to hear 'Jerusalem' on the Last Night of the Proms. It always makes the hair stand up on the back of my neck.

Picture courtesy BBC.

WHAT PIECE OF ADVICE WOULD YOU TAKE WITH YOU?

KEEP ATTACKING! Whenever things go wrong in life, just pick yourself up and keep attacking. Things will come good sooner or later.

Picture courtesy BBC.

WHICH CHILDHOOD MEMORY?

My parents moved around quite a lot when I was a child and I ended up going to nine different schools, so I was always the new kid on the block. Most of my memories therefore revolve around scrapping or kicking a football round the back streets of Liverpool.

TV PROGRAMME?

My favourite TV programme is 'Match of the Day'... but only when we win!

monster WORDSEARCH

In the grid below we have hidden no fewer than 25 Wolves heroes, past and present.

All the players or managers are listed below – can you find them?

```
S T A N C U L L I S R E W O L F N O R J
O Y X O U L E S S T E V E B U R P E O E
B I L L J E A Y A L E X R E A S N B L
E I M V P O B I L L Y W R I G H T A B L
R O I K A H J D O J O H A O N C E E I E
T D C E N N R O O B D S E J B H V K E W
W A K N E R E D I L N H T L I B E E D N
I V M N L I Y B I K I H C A R C B I E R
L P C Y L C T A A Q V S N T N T U B N A
L M C H U H M A T N E I E I U U L B N B
I A A I M A B J A C K W F N L M L O I N
A L R B Y R E O O R S S M D O U Y R S H
M C T B M D T A A D T C B C L J A D O O
S E H I M S R P R P A U L L N C E P N J
T I Y T I T K O Y X N D I L A B N V N A
E D L T J E S S E E B D A V K S E A R
V D A V R E T A L S L L I B R L E Y O D
D E R E K D O U G A N P A U L I N C E E
J O D Y C R A D D O C K E Y P E S S E J
Z G H Y E L K C U B K N A R F R O J A M
```

JOHN BARNWELL
EDDIE CLAMP
ROBBIE DENNISON
SYLVAN EBANKS-BLAKE
PAUL INCE
MICK MCCARTHY
DEREK PARKIN
JOHN RICHARDS
BILLY WRIGHT

MAJOR FRANK BUCKLEY
JODY CRADDOCK
DEREK DOUGAN
RON FLOWERS
DAVE JONES
JIMMY MULLEN
JESSE PYE
BILL SLATER

STEVE BULL
STAN CULLIS
KEVIN DOYLE
KENNY HIBBITT
ROBBIE KEANE
ANDY MUTCH
ALEX RAE
BERT WILLAMS

Answers on page 61!

22

MAKING HIS MARK

Mark Rhodes Interview

It's now eight years since a young and fresh-faced Midlander first burst onto the nation's television screens by finishing as runner-up in Pop Idol 2003. For Mark Rhodes, finishing second was the start rather than the end of a career which has since gone on from strength to strength.

Alongside fellow contestant Sam Nixon – who finished third that year – the pair have struck up a firm friendship and then working relationship, which has seen them enjoy great success initially in the pop charts and then in television and radio work.

Throughout the rollercoaster ride of the entertainment world however one thing has remained constant – Mark's love for Wolverhampton Wanderers. The Wolves Annual caught up with him to find out more...

Sam & Mark have become a deadly double act!

So Mark, how did your support of Wolves begin?

I was born and bred in Wolverhampton and it's my Dad's fault that I'm a Wolves fan as he brought me to my first game when I was eight or nine. It was against Bristol Rovers and Nigel Martyn was in goal. Steve Bull had about 1,000 chances to score but somehow Martyn just saved them all! It was still a fantastic occasion and from there I caught the Wolves bug.

Do you remember much of those early years?

Well, myself and my older brother then ended up having season tickets with my dad a few years after that first game. The first season was probably when we got into the play-offs and came up against Crystal Palace, but Dougie Freedman scored twice in the last minutes at Selhurst Park. We hammered them in the game back at Molineux, but only beat them 2-1 and went out on aggregate. I was devastated by that but it is still a season I remember.

Who was your Wolves hero?

It's got to be Bully. I know it's a cliché for supporters of my generation but it's true. There's nothing more you can say about Bully – he's a legend. I was also a massive fan of Mickey Stowell as well. He was an ever-present and got us out of some very sticky situations. I always thought he was a very under-rated keeper. I also have to mention Sir Jack Hayward, obviously if it wasn't for him we'd be out of business and I think every Wolves fan is grateful!

Did you play much yourself?

I tried to! I was left-footed which always helps in getting you into a few teams. It's like the old English problem. So I'd play left wing, left midfield, left back – anywhere down the left! I wasn't a pacey winger but I could put in a decent dead ball. I played a few seasons from when I was 11 to maybe 21/22 and it was good fun. When I realised I wasn't quite good enough to be a footballer I started singing!

Oh yes the singing – how did all that materialise?

I was about 16 maybe and started with a band at school. We got together and wrote original material and won a Midlands Battle of the Bands at the Robin 2 club in Bilston. We were able to record an album and it was all going well, but then, as happens in musical circles, there were differences of opinions and people not turning up to rehearsals. So it all ebbed away. But I really loved singing so I took out a loan, bought a lot of music gear (which I'm probably still paying off!), got a second hand car and did a lot of gigs around the Midlands. Having watched Pop Idol I just thought, why not? So I entered, and have been incredibly lucky ever since!

You've mentioned Bully. He was very supportive during Pop Idol wasn't he?

Yes he was. The first time I met Bully was when I'd got through to the final 50 of Pop Idol. They'd organised for him to be at the Wolves Retail Store because they knew I was a massive fan and wouldn't shut up about him. There were loads of cameras there and it was so surreal – he held up a Wolves shirt with the number '9' and 'Rhodes' on the back and presented it to me. There's a picture of me looking at him with the most bewildered 'stalker-ish' expression. I just told him 'You're my hero' – quite possibly the most stupid thing you could say to another human being without them being 'weirded' out! After that we became good friends and he and his wife Kirsty came down and supported me all the way through the shows. I'm very grateful to him and all the supporters I've had from the Midlands.

From there of course you teamed up with Sam – and the rest is history?!

It's another cliché but it's been a whirlwind eight years. It's been mad. Sam has been in my life all the way through my 20's. We met at the final 100 stage of Pop Idol and both had the same stupid sense of humour and got on really well. We actually said before we were put together that we should just go and live in London and see what happened. We finished second and third. I'm not going to say the music was the best ever to come out of Britain, but I think we could hold a tune and the TV stuff since has been fantastic. We have such a laugh and it really does beat working for a living.

Is Sam into football?

Not really. He came with me to Molineux and the Wolves training ground earlier this year and met Mick McCarthy who, like Sam, is from Barnsley. Mick was interested as soon as he knew Sam came from Barnsley and I couldn't understand a word each of them were saying! He's not into football and I do have a go at him for that sometimes because I do think that's weird. He's a bloke and doesn't like football – there's something wrong there. He's not having it though, he's into badminton. But I do love Mick McCarthy, for so many reasons. I imagine he can be a nightmare for journalists sometimes because he tells it like it is, but that's all in a good way. I think he's become Wolves through and through and you can tell how much the players respect him. That sort of togetherness has been vital during the tough times in the Premier League.

You certainly always seem keen to fly the flag for Wolves and the Midlands?

I always try and mention Wolves, even if no one wants to give me the chance to. I always try and mention them in a positive light because they

Where it all began – sitting in the stand with Dad Albert.

the Great North Run again, but not a Marathon. The training that goes into it is astronomical. But it was worth it for Whizz Kids because the people that are there work so hard, so anything we can do to help disabled children have a little bit more independence in their lives is fantastic. I managed to raise £10,000. Hopefully it will make a difference by buying three wheelchairs for three kids who need them.

Great stuff. And work-wise – has it been a busy year?

Yes it's been good. We started off the year with 'Comic Relief Does Glee Club' and then filmed another series of our quiz show Copycats. As you read this our brand new show 'Sam & Mark's Big Friday Wind Up' should either be on screen or just finished! It's a mixture of Beadle's About and Noel's House Party and we were really excited about doing it! We're also really busy with the radio show, which goes out over the whole of the Midlands on a Sunday between 11am and 1pm on BRMB, Wyvern, Mercia, Beacon and GEM 106. It's pretty awesome that all of my family who live around here get to listen, well only if they want to of course! They probably turn it off actually!

So life is generally pretty good at the moment?

Yes it is! Music and football have always been my two main passions in life. So to reach my goal with one of them and to support Wolves as well has been brilliant. I'm really looking forward to seeing Wolves again in the Premier League this season.

are my team. I'm really proud to support the club and have done all my life. It does get on my nerves when people say 'I used to support this team' and so on. You don't choose which team you support – you're born like it! And you support them through thick and thin. To be fair we've been on the 'up' for a long period of my lifetime thanks to Sir Jack Hayward, Steve Morgan and the work of Mick McCarthy and the current players. I still get to games whenever I can. I took my other half for the first time to Fulham last season and had to apologise at the end of the game as I got a bit excited! I'm just delighted we stayed in the Premier League last season and had another one to look forward to.

Looking back rather than forward, what has been your happiest ever Wolves memory?

My favourite memory without a shadow of a doubt was when I was lucky enough to get a ticket to the play-off final with Sheffield United. The first half of that game was just a blur to me. We were 3-0 up and it was game over. I kind of felt sorry for the Sheffield United fans because I was looking over and thinking they'd only just bought their pies and it was finished. It was such a great day, and I was so pleased for Dave Jones because I really rated him as a manager and as a person. That day was just incredible.

You've also done your bit this year by running the London Marathon in aid of the Whizz Kids wheelchair charity. What was all that about?

My nephew Tom used to play wheelchair football for Aston Villa. The last wheelchair he had before he passed away two years ago came from the Whizz Kids charity. Sam and I are patrons for Whizz Kids now which is incredible as we are the first to be asked and it's an honour. I did this year's London Marathon to raise money and have ticked it off the list now! I've got my medal – and I won't be doing it again! I'll do

'I was born under a Wanderers scarf.'

Keep an eye on Mark and what he's up to by visiting the Sam & Mark website – **www.samandmark.com** or follow the boys on twitter **www.twitter.com/samandmarktv**

picture perfect

It may have been a dramatic year on the pitch for the Wolves class of 2011 – but it was the same off it as well!

The squad were involved in a wide range of activities away from the football, both in support of the Wolves Community Trust charity as well as other important initiatives.

Here are a selection of pictures of the players out and about!

Stephen Hunt got behind Wolves' Kickz campaign by attending a netball session at Aldersley.

Jamie O'Hara at one of Wolves' Community Trust's Soccer Schools.

The Wolves Fashion Show, in conjunction with Harvey Nichols, proved another major success!

Adam Hammill and Jamie O'Hara cut some shapes at the Community Trust's Tackle Diabetes event.

Matt Murray and Kevin Doyle meet pupils from Bilston C of E Primary School at a 'Show Racism the Red Card event' at Molineux.

Keeper Marcus Hahnemann successfully completed his Private Pilot's License.

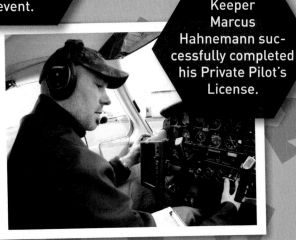

Santa Foley and Kevin Doyle meet two fans at the Young Wolves Christmas party.

Strikers Sylvan Ebanks-Blake and Steven Fletcher measure up at the launch of a major Wolves Community Trust campaign to 'Tackle Diabetes'.

Jody Craddock and Mick McCarthy at an art exhibition staged by Jody at Wolverhampton's Castle Galleries.

The pre-match walk before the Manchester City game took Wolves to Coronation Street and big fan Kevin Doyle is pictured outside the Rovers!

Club sponsors Sportingbet.com kindly let the players have a go at their half time challenge to raise funds for Wolves Community Trust.

Kevin Doyle with young Dylan Owen at New Cross Hospital, one of several Christmas visits carried out by the players.

MURRAY'S MINT
six of the best top tips

Popular former Wolves and England-under-21 keeper Matt Murray is enjoying a testimonial year in 2011, with events including a golf day, play-off reunion dinner and a match at Molineux.

The testimonial is raising money for four of Murray's chosen charities – Penn Hall School in Wolverhampton, the Alzheimer's Society, the Stroke Service Cycling Group from West Park Rehabilitation Hospital and Mzamowethu Pre-Primary School in South Africa.

Murray made an impressive impact during his career prior to being forced to hang up his gloves in August of 2010 due to continuing injury problems.

But he knows what it takes to make a professional career out of the game – and the qualities which are needed.

Here he offers six prime examples of the special qualities which can serve as an example to any youngster hoping to succeed, and players or managers who illustrate those qualities whom Murray worked with at Wolves.

IMPROVE YOUR TALENT

Robbie Keane

Robbie may be one of the most skilful players about, but that isn't all natural ability – he had to work at it as well.

When he was a kid his Mum used to set him challenges such as how long it would take him to get to the end of the street and back keeping the ball up.

Part of it was probably to get rid of him for a few minutes, but it all helped!

He is always doing extra work after training, as he has done throughout his career, even when I was with him as a young keeper at Wolves .

I remember being in goal after training when Robbie, David Connolly and Carl Robinson would always stay behind to work on their finishing.

If I was away on holiday with Robbie we'd always end up buying a ball and having a kick about – he could never get enough practice.

WANT TO BE THE BEST

Joleon Lescott

Joleon is someone who took everything on board when he was coming through at Wolves.

As a young player you don't always eat the most healthy food, but we all quickly realised that diet was important and Joleon in particular made sure he ate properly.

He's such a big and strong lad now and has an awesome build – probably the best on a footballer that I've seen.

Joleon is another who would work after training, for 15 or 20 minutes without fail with Terry Connor.

It was about improving his quality on the ball, making sure he could take the ball out either way and clear with either foot.

He wanted to be the very best player he possibly could, and also came back from a serious injury as well thanks to so much hard work.

NEVER LOSE MOTIVATION

Paul Ince/ Denis Irwin

Motivation and the will-to-win never deserts the very top players – and that's part of the reason why they stay at the top.

Money doesn't motivate.

Of course it's nice, and sometimes players want the finer things in life, but it when il came to Paul Ince and Denis Irwin, they helped us get promotion because they are both winners.

They would both give it their all, and play to win, in every single game.

Incey used to say to us before every game – "no regrets" – make sure you leave everything out on the pitch and then you can't ask any more than that.

Denis was slightly different, he led more by example, but also had massive standards out there on the pitch and made sure he met them every time he went out there.

LISTEN AND LEARN

Mike Stowell/ Michael Oakes

One of the biggest things for young players to remember is always to listen and learn.

And also to watch the other players in your position.

I'd always watch Mike Stowell and Michael Oakes in games, and other keepers like David James, not just with their saves but also positioning, even when the ball was at the other end of the pitch.

It's the same if you're a defender, midfielder or a striker.

It's always worth watching good players in that position to see what they do when they have got the ball and when they haven't.

You can always affect a game even if the ball is at the other end of the pitch.

It's so important to watch and listen because you can always learn, however good a player you are.

EXPRESS YOURSELF

Mick McCarthy

Amongst everything else it is also vital that young players enjoy playing the game.

The gaffer always said that to us from the moment he arrived at the club.

He told us not to be afraid and encouraged us to express ourselves on the pitch.

He told me to be positive, to come for crosses, and if I took 20 it didn't matter that I might then miss one.

It's about not making silly mistakes and taking unnecessary risks, but not being scared to try things, to get on the ball and take people on if that's your position.

The more you enjoy your football, and if you believe in yourself, the better you will be.

STAY LEVEL-HEADED

Jody Craddock

I think Jody Craddock is the best professional I have ever seen.

We were working in the gym once and he turned to me and said: "Do you know what Matty? I've had the best career I could possibly have had."

He always gives it his all and knows he couldn't have done any more – how awesome must it be to be able to say that?

When you do achieve any success it's important to stay level-headed, to 'keep it real', just like Jody does.

It's good to enjoy the things that come from football that you've worked hard for, but staying grounded is also crucial.

WHO SAID IT?

The 10 quotes below all came out of the mouths of Wolves' players, management or famous fans during the dramatic 2010/11 season.

Can you match the quote to the relevant speaker from the attached list? Answers on Page 61.

1 I can't believe the fuss about it. It's been blown out of all proportion and it's just because it was Joey Barton – if it was anyone else it probably wouldn't even have been mentioned.

2 I can't say enough about the manager's support – I could have been dropped and everyone would have understood that. The gaffer knows me and knows what I can do on the pitch and that I always give my best every training session and every game.

3 George needs to wind his neck in, it's my goal and I need to set the record straight. George is taking advantage of me being out of the country and trying to claim it while I'm not around to defend my corner.

I actually got a touch to it while being rugby tackled by George at the same time which is quite an achievement.

4 I've said to Steve Morgan – in the club shop next year we should have a Wolverhampton Wanderers pacemaker! It's always been hair-raising here and hopefully we've turned the corner now.

5 A football club like Wolves is steeped in history. All I am is the guy carrying the baton at this time.

It's like a long relay race, but I suppose like anyone who runs a relay you want to hand it over to someone in a better position than when you picked it up.

6 My phone has been going crazy and I couldn't get hold of my parents for a while.

I eventually phoned a restaurant where I thought they would be and fortunately they were there so I was able to tell them the news.

7 I can't explain how tough it's been for me over these last 16 months.

It's quite frightening the things I've gone through, mentally as well as physically, which is why I'm so pleased to be back on a pitch.

I haven't said this before but I did question it and I thought I might not play again.

8 There's a fair bit of pressure on it.

And it's quite a jump from starting out flying model aircraft to getting my licence within a year.

I took my wife up as my first passenger and now I'm responsible for the whole team!

It will be different but I'm sure it's going to be a lot of fun.

9 It didn't look like we were going to survive at half time.

Luckily we all stuck at it and I was just delighted to be able to come up with a goal.

I was on for a hat trick of relegations and it looked doomed again at half time.

But we managed to stick in there and were mentally strong and got back in the game.

10 I am thrilled and I am very proud of the players.

I am shattered physically and emotionally. I went through the wringer.

I feel like I should be dancing up and down swinging my drawers in the air.

I can't do that, because I have to stay professional, but that is how I feel.

MOLINEUX'S First Lady!

It was in November, 2010, that the news broke that Wolves Vice-President Rachael Heyhoe Flint had been elevated into the House of Lords as a Conservative working peer.

But to those connected with Wolves, and indeed the city of Wolverhampton, Rachael had already been the First Lady of Molineux for many many years!

Baroness Heyhoe Flint of Wolverhampton – as is now her correct title – has enjoyed a lifelong association with her home city and the football club which she has served in so many different ways over the past few decades.

And now, that staunch affiliation can be shared and discussed – in the Upper Chamber of the Westminster Parliament!

"It can be very pleasing in the Upper House to look across to the Opposition benches and see Lord Bilston (Dennis Turner), also of course from Wolverhampton," she says.

"Every Monday during the footie season we will bump into one another in the Peers' lobby and conversation could be either 'can you believe that happened' or 'what a great result that was'!

Freedom of the City of Wolverhampton!

Inducted into the House of Lords.

Then there's Lord Grocutt (Bruce Grocutt), who is a big Stoke fan, and Lord Grade (Michael Grade), who supports Charlton – and even the Lord Speaker, Baroness Helene Hayman, is a former Wolverhampton Girls High School pupil and loves Wolves, even though her sons are Arsenal fans!

There can sometimes be as much talk about football as politics!

I remember the Monday after we achieved Premier League survival despite losing to Blackburn on the last day of the season – so many peers and doorkeepers and attendants were telling me how they had been watching events unfold and had been rooting for us.

Every football fan is the same whichever football team you support; you always go through the whole range of emotions whether good or bad results emerge.

It's like what happened on the final day of last season, so many fluctuations in the 90 minutes. In all my decades of playing and watching sport – I hadn't ever experienced anything like that before. We were relegated for 17 minutes – that was ghastly – but praise be to Stephen Hunt and even Pavyluchenko of Spurs for their life-saving goals!"

The good ship Wolverhampton Wanderers has clearly played a major part in the life of Rachael, in many other sport and business pursuits and charitable enterprises.

The indefatigable 72-year-old's earliest memory of Wolves is recalling the 1949 FA Cup Wembley triumph against Leicester, at a time when her parents were both season ticket holders at Molineux. "We watched on our neighbours TV in Penn – we couldn't afford a television," she says.

Her father, a very capable gymnast, was a physical education teacher who became

Director of Physical Education for Wolverhampton; he also lectured at the Technical College on the site of the Wolverhampton University Reception in Wulfruna Street.

One of those who used to attend Geoffrey Heyhoe's Technical College evening keep fit classes was a young chap by the name of William Ambrose Wright.

"I used to say that the reason Billy Wright could jump higher than anyone else was because of my Dad," says Lady Heyhoe Flint with a chuckle.

Those early Wolves links, coupled with her own love of sport, meant that trips to Molineux quickly became a regular feature of life for the Wolverhampton Girls High pupil, born in Claregate.

"I'd go with my brother, and we'd stand in the Cowshed," she recalls.

A cricketing trailblazer.

"My brother used to take a building brick to stand on which we took into the ground in a hessian bag made by my mum.

I'm not sure nowadays if my brother's explanation of the brick being used so that his sister could see the game is one that would get you into the ground today!"

It wasn't just Billy Wright with whom the Heyhoe Flint family enjoyed a close association.

When Lady Heyhoe Flint's father became Director of Physical Education for all of Wolverhampton, he used to purchase a lot of equipment from legendary Wolves and England keeper Bert Williams, who had two shops at the time.

"The shop at Bilston also had a warehouse which included a cricket net and my Dad used to take me to Bert's net to coach me", adds Lady Heyhoe Flint.

"I also worked at Bert's Wolverhampton shop for a couple of years from when I was 16 to earn some pocket money, and I remember Bert heading off on a Saturday morning to play for Wolves and then coming back in the evening to close up!"

It wasn't long before Lady Heyhoe-Flint's own sporting prowess started to come to the fore.

Over two decades as a regular in the England Women's cricket team, 12 years of that as

A very young RHF – complete with dolly!

skipper, her roll of honour with bat and ball included captaining the team to victory in the inaugural World Cup of 1973, remaining unbeaten in six Test series and notching three test centuries, one of which – a knock of 179 against the Aussies at the Oval in 1976 – was a world record at the time.

There was also the small matter of representing her country at hockey and playing one of her four international appearances as England's goalkeeper at Wembley Stadium. "I played in goal because I wanted to be like Bert Williams – my hero!"

But it was via her cricketing career that she first made contact with a certain Sir Jack Hayward, thus creating a situation which would not only benefit England ladies' cricket, but later see her take a far more active role at Molineux.

A letter written to Sir Jack's father, Charles, seeking sponsorship for a tour of West Indies in 1969 found its way – via Charles's wastepaper basket – into the hands of the future Wolves owner.

"Amazingly Sir Jack agreed to sponsor our tour – "he said he was happy to support a fellow Wulfrunian – and a successful England cricket team!"

Sir Jack also sponsored the first ever Cricket World Cup, for men or women, in 1973.

"Jack became a great family friend from there, and I always knew how keen he was to get involved at Wolves," adds Lady Heyhoe-Flint.

"He sadly missed out by five minutes with a bid to buy the Club in 1982 when the Bhatti Brothers took over, and it was so wonderful when he finally bought the club in 1990.

I then got a phone call from Sir Jack asking me to come and work for the club and, later on, in

1997, he invited me to join the Board, which was an incredible honour, for six years.

At the time I had moved from teaching PE (from 1960) into Journalism and Public Relations in 1965, so to get the chance to work for the club I loved was wonderful."

Both before and during her close connection with Wolves, Rachael has deservedly collected a raft of honours for her work in sport, charity and the community.

Her elevation to the House of Lords place was preceded by the award of an MBE in 1972 and OBE in 2008, and she also became a Deputy Lieutenant of the West Midlands in 1997 for services to sport and charity.

In cricket, Rachael was the first woman to be elected to the full committee of the MCC at Lords in 1994 and then first woman inducted into the ICC Cricket Hall of Fame in October, 2010.

Honorary degrees have been collected from the Universities of Wolverhampton, Leeds Metropolitan, Bradford and Greenwich.

"Ironic really because my academic career at school and Physical Education College were marked by examination failures!" she says.

"I spent too much time playing sport rather than studying".

The Freedom of the City of Wolverhampton was awarded to Rachael earlier this year.

Then there's the extensive charity work, carried out by Rachael with the Lord's and Lady Taverners Charity in addition to all that she has undertaken in and around Wolverhampton through Wolves' registered charity Wolves Aid.

The honours however do not change Lady Heyhoe Flint – in the words of Mick McCarthy she will probably always remain "Our Rachael" to those that know her.

She is quick to deflect any personal accolades derived from her charitable work to that carried out by Wolves Aid – now part of Wolves Community Trust – of which she is one of six trustees.

"The Club had a very small Community Department back in 1990, but Wolves Community Trust is now a really vibrant 'giving' organisation," she explains.

"I would definitely say that a lot of the personal recognition I have had has been due to the community work we have undertaken with Wolves over the last 20 years through Wolves Aid.

"We have worked with Power Pleas, the Wolverhampton wheelchair charity, and very proudly the club and the fans have provided 17 wheelchairs in the last 16 years for special needs youngsters to improve their quality of life.

WCT also devised the Dusk/Midnight/Twilight league where we encourage local needy youngsters to kick a football rather than kicking in a door or a window. Wolves Community Trust provides the coaches and the facilities.

I have to reveal myself as a Conservative, but when the current Government were in opposition I managed to get David Cameron, Hugh Robertson (now Minister for Sport) and Jeremy Hunt (Secretary of State for Culture, Media and Sport) to Molineux to look at the work of the DTM League.

This project demonstrates the corporate social responsibility undertaken by Wolves FC; our work has become a model for many others in the Football League.

I'm convinced it is such community initiatives and so much more at Wolves which has taken me to those famous red leather benches in the House of Lords!"

From one Lords (the Test cricket ground) to another, the journey taken by Rachael is one which remains inextricably linked with Wolverhampton Wanderers.

In typically animated pose with Sue Barker at Molineux.

"When I was choosing my title I wondered if I could be Baroness Heyhoe Flint of Molineux – but that is a hereditary French family name so I chose Baroness Heyhoe Flint of Wolverhamptom... although in my mind I add Wanderers Football Club!"

Supported all the way by husband Derrick and family, who are all great Wolves fans, she is clearly thrilled by her latest appointment, admitting: "The House of Lords is a remarkable place and I am really enjoying it. There is so much to learn, particularly coming from a non-political background – but I shall never forget my roots!"

PLAYER PROFILES

JODY CRADDOCK

POSITION: Defender
BORN: Redditch, 25/07/75
FORMER CLUBS: Cambridge, Sunderland, Sheffield United (loan), Stoke (loan)
JOINED WOLVES: July, 2003
HIGHLIGHT: Winning Wolves' Player of the Season award for 2009/10 campaign.

CARL IKEME

POSITION: Goalkeeper
BORN: Birmingham, 08/06/86
FORMER CLUBS: Accrington Stanley, Stockport, Charlton, Sheffield United, QPR, Leicester (all loans)
JOINED WOLVES: July, 2003 (signed pro)
HIGHLIGHT: Keeping a clean sheet on his Wolves league debut in a 2-0 win against Bristol City.

WAYNE HENNESSEY

POSITION: Goalkeeper
BORN: Anglesey, 24/01/87
FORMER CLUBS: Bristol City, Stockport (both loans)
JOINED WOLVES: April, 2005 (signed pro)
HIGHLIGHT: Being named Wolves Player of the Year and in PFA Championship Team of the Year in 2008.

KARL HENRY

POSITION: Midfielder
BORN: Wolverhampton, 26/11/82
FORMER CLUBS: Stoke, Cheltenham (loan)
JOINED WOLVES: July, 2006
HIGHLIGHT: Being named in a provisional senior England squad in February, 2011.

MICHAEL KIGHTLY

POSITION: Winger

BORN: Basildon, 24/01/86

FORMER CLUBS: Southend, Farnborough (loan), Grays Athletic

JOINED WOLVES: November, 2006

HIGHLIGHT: Making England-under-21 debut against Romania in August, 2007.

ANDY KEOGH

POSITION: Striker

BORN: Dublin, 16/05/86

FORMER CLUBS: Leeds, Bury (loan), Scunthorpe, Bristol City, Cardiff (last two loans)

JOINED WOLVES: January, 2007

HIGHLIGHT: Scored the first Republic of Ireland goal of Giovanni Trapattoni's reign, which also earned the Irish Goal of the Year award for 2008.

STEPHEN WARD

POSITION: Everywhere (except in goal!)

BORN: Dublin, 20/08/85

FORMER CLUBS: Bohemians

JOINED WOLVES: January, 2007

HIGHLIGHT: Scoring the winning goal in Wolves' first win at Liverpool for 27 years in December, 2010.

MATT JARVIS

POSITION: Winger

BORN: Middlesbrough, 22/05/86

FORMER CLUBS: Millwall, Gillingham

JOINED WOLVES: June, 2007

HIGHLIGHT: Becoming Wolves' first England international for over 20 years against Ghana in March, 2011.

PLAYER PROFILES

KEVIN FOLEY

POSITION: Defender/Midfielder
BORN: Luton, 01/11/84
FORMER CLUBS: Luton
JOINED WOLVES: August, 2007
HIGHLIGHT: Proud to captain Wolves for the first time in the Barclays Premier League – and score – in the home win against Sunderland in November, 2010.

DAVE EDWARDS

POSITION: Midfielder
BORN: Shrewsbury, 03/02/86
FORMER CLUBS: Shrewsbury, Luton
JOINED WOLVES: January, 2008
HIGHLIGHT: Scored the winner as Wolves earned their first win over one of the top flight 'big boys' in beating Manchester City in October, 2010.

SYLVAN EBANKS-BLAKE

POSITION: Striker
BORN: Cambridge, 29/03/86
FORMER CLUBS: Manchester United, Royal Antwerp (loan), Plymouth
JOINED WOLVES: January, 2008
HIGHLIGHT: Named Championship Player of the Year for 2009 at the end of two seasons in which he had won the Golden Boot.

GEORGE ELOKOBI

POSITION: Defender
BORN: Cameroon, 31/01/86
FORMER CLUBS: Colchester, Chester (loan)
JOINED WOLVES: January, 2008
HIGHLIGHT: Being called up to the Cameroon squad for the first time for a training camp in November, 2010.

SAM VOKES

POSITION: Striker

BORN: Southampton,21/10/89

FORMER CLUBS: Bournemouth, Leeds, Bristol City, Sheffield United, Norwich (last four loans)

JOINED WOLVES: May, 2008

HIGHLIGHT: Equaliser against Plymouth on the opening day of the 2008/09 season helped Wolves secure the first point of their Championship winning season.

RICHARD STEARMAN

POSITION: Defender

BORN: Wolverhampton, 19/08/87

FORMER CLUBS: Leicester

JOINED WOLVES: June, 2008

HIGHLIGHT: Turned out for England-Under-21s in the European Championships of 2009, playing the full game in a draw with eventual winners Germany.

CHRISTOPHE BERRA

POSITION: Defender

BORN: Edinburgh, 31/01/85

FORMER CLUBS: Heart of Midlothian

JOINED WOLVES: January, 2009

HIGHLIGHT: Ended long wait for first international goal by heading home for Scotland against Wales in the Carling Nations Cup tie of May, 2011.

NENAD MILIJAŠ

POSITION: Midfielder

BORN: Serbia, 30/04/83

FORMER CLUBS: FK Zemun, Red Star Belgrade

JOINED WOLVES: June, 2009

HIGHLIGHT: Proved a man for the big occasion in the 2010/11 season, scoring against Manchester City both home and away.

PLAYER PROFILES

KEVIN DOYLE

POSITION: Striker
BORN: Adamstown, 18/09/83
FORMER CLUBS: Cork City, Reading
JOINED WOLVES: June, 2009
HIGHLIGHT: Received a double international awards success in February 2011 with the Republic of Ireland Player of the Year and Goal of the Year accolades.

RONALD ZUBAR

POSITION: Defender
BORN: Guadeloupe, 20/09/85
FORMER CLUBS: Caen, Marseille
JOINED WOLVES: June, 2009
HIGHLIGHT: Scored first Premier League goal on a superb night for Wolves as they won 3-1 at West Ham in March, 2010.

ADLENE GUEDIOURA

POSITION: Midfielder
BORN: France, 12/11/85
FORMER CLUBS: RSC Charleroi
JOINED WOLVES: January, 2010
HIGHLIGHT: Returned from a broken leg towards the end of the 2010/11 season and scored a crucial goal in the Black Country derby win against West Bromwich Albion.

STEVEN FLETCHER

POSITION: Striker
BORN: Shrewsbury, 26/03/87
FORMER CLUBS: Hibernian, Burnley
JOINED WOLVES: June, 2010
HIGHLIGHT: Became the first Wolves player since John Richards to score ten top flight league goals in a season in his first campaign at Molineux.

STEPHEN HUNT

POSITION: Winger
BORN: Portlaoise, 01/08/81
JOINED WOLVES: June, 2010
FORMER CLUBS: Crystal Palace, Brentford, Reading, Hull
HIGHLIGHT: Scored the crucial goal at Blackburn which effectively pushed Wolves into surviving on the dramatic final day of the 2010/11 campaign.

ADAM HAMMILL

POSITION: Winger
BORN: Liverpool, 25/01/88
JOINED WOLVES: January, 2011
FORMER CLUBS: Liverpool, Dunfermline (loan), Southampton (loan), Blackpool (loan), Barnsley
HIGHLIGHT: Shortly after joining Wolves, made his England-Under-21 debut against Iceland at Preston.

JAMIE O'HARA

POSITION: Midfielder
BORN: Dartford, 25/09/86
JOINED WOLVES: January, 2011 (initially on loan)
FORMER CLUBS: Tottenham, Chesterfield (loan), Millwall (loan), Portsmouth (loan)
HIGHLIGHT: First Wolves goal against West Bromwich Albion earned the club's Goal of the Season award for 2010/11.

LEIGH GRIFFITHS

POSITION: Striker
BORN: Leith, 20/08/90
JOINED WOLVES: January, 2011
FORMER CLUBS: Livingstone, Dundee
HIGHLIGHT: A glut of goals for Dundee included a 30-yard free kick against Rangers in the quarter finals of the Scottish Cup.

PLAYER PROFILES

DORUS DE VRIES

POSITION: Goalkeeper
BORN: Beverwijk, 29/12/80
JOINED WOLVES: June, 2011
FORMER CLUBS: Telstar, Den Haag, Dunfermline, Swansea
HIGHLIGHT: Playing in all of Swansea's league games in the promotion-winning 2010/11 season, culminating in the play-off final win against Reading at Wembley.

ROGER JOHNSON

POSITION: Defender
BORN: Ashford, 28/04/83.
JOINED WOLVES: July, 2011
FORMER CLUBS: Wycombe, Cardiff, Birmingham
HIGHLIGHT: Part of the Birmingham team who defeated Arsenal in the 2011 Carling Cup Final and played a part in the opening goal of the 2-1 win.

STEFAN MAIERHOFER

POSITION: Striker
BORN: Gablitz, 16/08/82
JOINED WOLVES: August, 2009
FORMER CLUBS: SV Langenrohr, Bayern Munich, TuS Koblenz, Rapid Vienna, Bristol City (loan), MSV Duisburg (loan).
HIGHLIGHT: Netted on his Wolves debut after coming off the bench against Blackburn and also for Duisburg in a German Cup Semi Final.

the young PROFESSIONALS

AARON McCAREY
Goalkeeper

DANNY BATTH
Defender

SCOTT MALONE
Defender

JAMIE RECKORD
Defender

ETHAN EBANKS-LANDELL
Defender

MATT DOHERTY
Defender

DAVID DAVIS
Midfielder

LOUIS HARRIS
Midfielder

ANTHONY FORDE
Midfielder

JACK PRICE
Midfielder

NATHANIEL MENDEZ-LAING
Winger

JOHNNY GORMAN
Winger

ZELI ISMAIL
Winger

LIAM MCALINDEN
Striker

JAMES SPRAY
Striker

SAM WINNALL
Striker

ASHLEY HEMMINGS
Striker

JAKE CASSIDY
Striker

JEZ GETS HIS KICKS!

For many people, the chance to unwind after a long, hard day at the office would probably mean a nice cuppa in front of the television, a nose in a good book or maybe popping out for an evening stroll.

Not so Wolves Chief Executive Jez Moxey.

No. When Moxey wants to escape from the stresses and strains of life at the helm of a Barclays Premier League club there's usually only one thing on his mind.

Karate.

A self confessed 'football suit', the need for Wolves' 48-year-old CEO to be able to let off steam amid the intensity of a job in which physical exercise is at a premium is paramount.

He has found that release, via regular weekly trips to the Dudley Shukokai Karate Club, which meets at Thorns Community College in Brierley Hill.

As Moxey explains, karate is a martial art which he has practised – on and off – for the best part of two decades.

"When I was working with Partick Thistle many years ago we were in the process of building the new East Stand," he explains.

"Glasgow was a great experience for me, but it's quite a tough place and I felt I needed to get some stress relief from the job I was doing.

A friend of mine joined a karate club and suggested I went along – and immediately I caught the bug.

I carried on with the karate during my time with Rangers up until the time I joined Stoke City, by which time I had reached the level of 3rd Kyu Brown Belt, which was the first Brown Belt.

On moving to Stoke (in 1995), I tried to find a karate club once or twice, but when I found one I didn't like it and then my family and my career took over.

So it wasn't until maybe three-and-a-half years ago that I thought I should take it up again and found the Dudley Shukokai Karate Club.

I went there, enjoyed it, and have been going two or three times a week ever since."

Moxey's knowledge of sports and high level competition extends far beyond the pressurised environment of the other side of an office desk or

41

indeed cheering Wolves on from the Directors' Box, either at Molineux or across the country.

A top basketball player in his youth, he reached the status of Under-21 honours with England, played ten years as a professional, and has always clearly relished the spirit of competition.

"Being a competitive type of person, karate lends itself perfectly to me," he adds.

"It's a physical exercise, a competitive exercise and a really disciplined sport.

It teaches you respect, control and skills, whilst at the same time helping improve your fitness and learning a martial art which generally improves people's confidence and self belief.

It's a great physical release, not only mentally challenging but physically as well, which is really important in my job.

The club I go to is fabulous in that it's really mixed, with kids as young as five all the way up to old codgers like me, from all sorts of walks of life and backgrounds.

Whilst there are some people interested in football, I go to the Dudley Shukokai Karate Club as Jez the karate student, with people interested in me for my karate rather than the football.

That's a big release for me, to go there and not be Jez Moxey the football suit, but just Jez Moxey the person amongst really good people learning Shukokai style karate.

Once or twice a week during the season and maybe two to four times a week during the close season, this is my two hours to go to karate and temporarily put Wolves and football out of my mind.

And it's a really great way of recharging my mental batteries as well as challenging this old out-of-shape body of mine.

So if anyone has got a bone to pick with me then come and join our karate club, and let's have the disagreement settled on the Dojo!

I say that tongue in cheek, but I would certainly recommend karate and the club in particular; it has been fabulous for me.

It's a really family-orientated and happy club and is highly successful not only in the competitions but in terms have having students representing FEKO (the England team) in international tournaments around the world."

Moxey himself has entered a couple of competitions representing the Dudley club – and on one occasion it didn't exactly go to plan.

Indeed the phrase 'No Pain No Gain' might have been particularly apt after one showdown with a rather accurate opponent!

"I have competed twice in competitions," he explains.

"You can either enter 'Kata' class, which is the pre-determined karate moves where judges grade you on a points scoring basis, and/or there is actual fighting.

"For my two competitions I participated in veterans' fighting, which is a step-up again in terms of the adrenalin rush to be face to face with someone you have never seen before!

It's not quite 'mortal combat' though you do get into serious combative fighting with self control, but the medics always seem to be busy!

And in the last competition, although I won the silver medal, I was left with a very bruised chin after receiving a rather uncontrolled 'Gyakuzuki' (punch) to the face - or maybe I just didn't move quick enough to avoid it!

But those sort of things happen which is part and parcel of this great sport."

A painful kick or punch to the face aside, Moxey has, however, enjoyed some success in his pursuit of karate improvement.

And indeed, earlier this year he reached what many adjudge to be the pinnacle of the art – finally acquiring his Black Belt.

However, he views that as just the beginning of the next stage of his karate development.

"In the summer I graded and managed to pass my First Dan," he adds.

That gives me the Black Belt.

For the uninitiated – as I was when I first started karate – I thought reaching the Black Belt meant you were the finished product.

But in reality, reaching First Dan is just the beginning of it.

You've sort of served your apprenticeship, got the basic skills and from now onwards you can move up to, I think, Ninth Dan.

Our chief instructor or 'Sensei' is a 5th Dan and a former World Champion, and while you wouldn't immediately think it I wouldn't pick a fight with her!

She'd kick my backside with ease even though she is about 5ft 5' and less than 70 kilos.

We have other students and assistant instructors who are second, third and fourth Dan who regularly represent FEKO and I think they are brilliant.

So there is a long long way to go before I would feel I've become really proficient at this sport."

Karate is not the only 'release' for Moxey, though when he is able to grab the odd minute or two away from the fairly unrelenting glare of Wolves and the Premier League.

Describing himself as a "fair weather biker", he enjoys the "adrenalin rush" of getting out on his

Honda VFR 800 motorbike, having passed his test during his tenure in the Potteries, and regularly takes his convertible Jag out for a drive through the country lanes of Shropshire.

He has also been pounding the streets without the aid of any horsepower this year as he trained for the 13 miles half marathon of the Bupa Great North Run, which he, and several Wolves directors, were due to take on for charity in Newcastle in September.

Any other breaks away from the office are designated family time with wife Babette and four children, who get away whenever possible to a holiday home in Florida.

Having said 'holiday' home, the time difference means Moxey is usually found at his laptop or on the mobile phone during the mornings before being able to switch off in the afternoon as evening falls in the UK.

Switching off, however, is certainly not something he can afford to do on the Dojo, and, even with the Black Belt now secured, Wolves' CEO is keen to continue getting his kicks from karate for many years to come.

Anyone interested in joining Jez at Dudley Shukokai Karate Club can do so by contacting Sensei Mandie Read on **07979 461229** or visit **www.dudleyshukokai.co.uk** for details.

JOHNNY GORMAN cool for school!

There have been times in the last 18 months when Johnny Gorman has been the most talked about schoolboy since Harry Potter!

But the only tricks and spells the Wolves wing wizard is interested in are those that can take him past any non-suspecting full back as he now embarks on his main career ambition – to be a professional footballer.

The last two years have seen Gorman occupy the fairly ground-breaking position of combining studying for his A-levels at the prestigious Repton School in Derbyshire with his life as a full-time scholar at Molineux.

What has added even more interest to the mix has been the fact that the winger – who turns 19 in October, 2011 – also became a fully-fledged Northern Ireland international right in the middle of those studies in PE, Art and English Literature.

In winning his first cap against Turkey in May 2010, Sheffield-born Gorman, whose mother Su was born in Coleraine, became the seventh youngest player ever to represent Northern Ireland – outdoing even George Best by over 100 days!

By the end of the summer of 2011 he had amassed no fewer than eight caps, leaving him heading into his first season as a professional at Molineux with a fair bit of big game experience already under his belt.

So a student, aspiring footballer – and international footballer to boot – little wonder he became the focus of plenty of attention.

Does he now feel something of a figurehead – making it cool to be at school?!

"People had said to me when I first joined Repton that I could be the first person to do this of many," says Gorman.

That I could be seen as the one who made the breakthrough on the educational side of football.

There aren't many players in the Premier League or any level who carry on their education, but if you look at the French players, some of them still study and have got degrees!

It wasn't just about going to school and doing the A-levels though, I have met good and helpful people at Repton, it's also been about life experience.

There are others coming through now who are planning on doing exactly the same as I have done, either with another club or around the area.

So hopefully I've made a breakthrough."

Talking of breakthroughs, that international bow coming as it did so soon into his career clearly threw the spotlight on Gorman's education/football combination.

The former Manchester United trainee admits it made for an incredible year, and harbours no regrets whatsoever about the decision that he took.

From a family where mother Su and father Mike are both heavily involved in education, he was always well aware of the value of a solid foundation and back-up for the end of his football career, whenever that might be.

"If I hadn't got a pro contract I would have been left with nothing to fall back on and just felt it was too much of a risk not to carry on," he says.

"Coming from a

In action for Wolves Development squad during a tour of Northern Ireland.

family background where both my parents are university lecturers, they guided me towards education – although it was my final decision and I wanted to do it.

Repton were very helpful and flexible.

It was a pretty incredible year all-round, picking up eight caps and doing my A-levels .

If someone had told me that would happen I'd never have believed them."

Gorman is also grateful to the support of Wolves Academy and Development structures which, via Kevin Thelwell and Steve Weaver, helped nurture him through the last two years to secure a new professional contract.

Named Young Player of the Year last season, he headed into the current campaign keen to follow in the footsteps of other Academy graduates before him, whether that be by continuing to impress at reserve team level or being despatched on loan to build up experience elsewhere.

A historic Northern Ireland debut against Turkey.

It's all about catching the eye of boss Mick McCarthy, albeit with the knowledge that there are now far fewer players breaking into Premier League teams at 17 or 18 than say 21 or 22.

"I was in the matchday squad against Birmingham last season and had a squad number without making the bench, but again it was a great experience," he recalls.

"It's something that will hopefully help me if I do get in a squad because I've had that little bit of experience.

It was always going to be unrealistic to try and break through while I was studying.

I'm not going to lie – of course I'd have wanted to have played if I could – but I wasn't there half the week and was doing my A-levels.

Johnny in his Repton uniform with a piece of his A-level artwork.

I was fairly happy playing for the reserves and the Academy and scoring a few goals and having a pleasing season.

The one thing that stood out for me was a 'stat' I heard when I was about 15.

It said that one player in five from that age would stay in the game until they were 21 and that's in any league, not necessarily the Premier League.

For me that was such an overwhelming stat and made my mind up that I needed to do my education. I do have time on my side because there are a lot of players now breaking through at 20 and 21 not 17 and 18.

Once I completed my A-levels though it was time to come back this season and be 100 per cent focused on football – and I genuinely couldn't wait!

It's all about keeping my feet on the ground with everything, working as hard as possible, and hopefully impressing the gaffer."

BULLY'S BEST

Bully with strike partner Andy Mutch.

It may be over 12 years now since the legend that is Stephen George Bull hung up his boots.

But Wolves' Vice President and record goalscorer remains as keen a supporter of the club as he ever was.

You certainly can't beat a bit of Bully – but what of his own thoughts and memories of the Beautiful Game?

The Wolves Annual caught up with the great man to discover the list of Bully's Best – players and memories which he puts at the top of his career.

Read on to find out more!

BEST GOAL

I genuinely haven't really got a favourite one! I always said that my best goals were with my left foot, because that was my standing leg and if you take that away I fell over. I did score over 100 goals with my left foot so any of them will do. There's one from 25 yards against Bury I scored with my left foot at Molineux, so that one probably stands out. But I enjoyed them all!

BEST GAME

It's got to be Newcastle away at St James's Park on New Year's Day, 1990. I scored four goals in the second half and we won 4-1. We'd had a few beers in the hotel the night before. We shouldn't have, and we only did it once, but it worked! It was a really memorable day and I remember the fans all going up there on the plane and many dressed as Santa or reindeers. It was the start of the World Cup year and I think Bobby Robson was watching in the stands at the time.

BEST INDIVIDUAL PERFORMANCE

Portsmouth away. Mutchy (Andy Mutch) was sent off and I had to run the front-line all game. The gaffer (Graham Turner) said that was the best performance he'd seen from a lone striker because I was running and chasing and scored as well.

BEST PLAYER PLAYED WITH

I'd go for a couple but on a Wolves level it would have to be Mutchy. We had a great understanding on the pitch, even though we couldn't understand what each other was saying! He was the provider and I was the goalscorer. I think he was probably a bit underestimated by the fans in terms of what he did for the club. The other I'd say would be Paul Gascoigne when I played for England. He was pure class and really opened my eyes to how good he was when I joined up with the squad. He also set up my two goals against Czechoslavakia.

BEST PLAYER PLAYED AGAINST

The toughest opponent would be Gerry Taggart. We had some right old battles. He was a man mountain and I just couldn't get around him. I was used to getting away from defenders and getting a shot in but Gerry Taggart was everywhere with his body or an elbow! The best defender I played against was Des Walker. He was the quickest and most nimble defender I ever faced. When we were against Nottingham Forest I'd get away from him and think I was away, but then he was so fast he'd be back and wrapping his leg around the ball.

Firing home against Czechoslavakia.

BEST MANAGER

I'd have to thank Nobby Stiles and Johnny Giles for discovering me at Albion but then I'd say Graham Turner at Wolves. The seven years I had with him at Wolves after he signed me were absolutely superb and he was such a great man manager. I'd also throw in Bobby Robson with England. He was a top man and another great man manager who treated everyone the same whatever their background.

With Graham Turner (right).

BEST TEAM PERFORMANCE

As a collective? Would probably have to be against the Albion when we beat them 4-2 at The Hawthorns in 1996. It's often difficult in a local derby for every single player to shine, but that's what happened on that day. That was one of the best team performances I was involved in and we blew them away in the first half hour.

BEST ENGLAND MOMENT

It would have to be Hampden Park and my debut. There were over 80,000 there and of the 6,000 England fans I think 3,000 were from Wolves. It was all about 'Let the Bull loose' and 'Bully's gonna get ya!' For me to go on and score on my international debut was one of the best memories of my career and I could talk about it all day long. It was my big breakthrough and a year later I was off to the World Cup.

BEST WOLVES JOKER

There were a few to be fair. If I was going to pick one it would be David 'Digger' Barnes who played at left back. He was a comic and absolutely superb. There were so many stories. I remember the once when Graham Turner was giving everyone a rollocking and throwing cups all over the place. Digger had some black tape on his teeth and just looked up and grinned and we all burst out laughing. Graham stormed out and Digger had to follow him to his office. There was such a great team spirit in those days and we had some great times. We were all pranksters in our own way.

STEVE BULL FOUNDATION

Steve is very proud to have launched his own charity last year – The Steve Bull Foundation.

"I have been involved in charitable work for many years and have been a Patron of a locally based national charity - Promise Dreams since it began in 2001. That work will continue.

However, my profile meant that I was getting so many requests to help different charities that I decided to put all my charity work under one umbrella. It was a dream come true when I was finally able to launch my own Foundation in August last year with a party at the Molineux with my old mate Robert Plant performing live.

My Foundation will provide charitable support in the form of grants to organisations primarily in the Black Country and the West Midlands which specialise in assisting young people, the disabled, the homeless, the sick and the disadvantaged."

BEST ROOM-MATE

Thommo (Andy Thompson). He was my room-mate for seven years from when we joined the club together. I always used to like the bottom bunk but he had to have it because he couldn't get up the ladder to the top. He was top drawer and we always had great banter – we were like each other's shadows. We're still in touch as we are with all the former players.

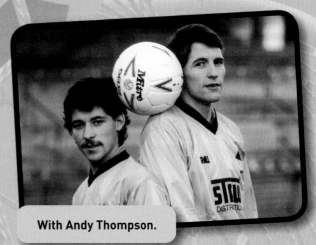

With Andy Thompson.

BEST THING ABOUT FOOTBALL

Just that it's football. Everybody loves football don't they? Why? I don't know. Maybe the banter, the excitement, the camaraderie. Being at a football ground and watching a game with the atmosphere is just fantastic.

the NUMBERS game

All of the questions below refer to events of the 2010/11 season and are in some way connected to numbers.

1 Mick McCarthy's 200th game in charge of Wolves came towards the start of the 2010/11 season. Who was it against?

(a) Newcastle   (b) Everton
(c) Fulham

2 Matt Jarvis became the first Wolves player in over two decades to win a senior England cap. What number did he wear?

(a) 15   (b) 16   (c) 17

3 Wolves' highest crowd of the season at Molineux was 29, 086. But who was the game against?

(a) Manchester United (b) Blackburn
(c) Blackpool

4 Which Wolves player celebrated his 25th birthday on the final day of the season?

(a) Kevin Foley   (b) Matt Jarvis
(c) Stephen Ward

5 Wolves attracted a lot of attention for a so-called physical approach to matches in the early stages of the season. But where did they finish in the Barclays Premier League's Fair Play Table?

(a) 10th   (b) 13th   (c) 16th

6 Steven Fletcher finished as Wolves top scorer in all competitions. But how many did he get in the league?

(a) 10   (b) 11   (c) 12

7 Wolves scored and conceded exactly the same amount of goals in their home games. How many?

(a) 25   (b) 30   (c) 35

8 Wolves average attendance in league games over the season was 27,696. Where did that see them finish in the attendance table?

(a) 10th   (b) 12th   (c) 14th

9 How many clean sheets did Wolves keep in the league?

(a) 3   (b) 4   (c) 5

10 Matt Jarvis appeared in most Barclays Premier League games for Wolves – 37 of the 38. Who was the next most-used player with 34 appearances?

(a) Stephen Ward (b) Christophe Berra
(c) Kevin Foley

11 If matches had finished at half time, where would Wolves have finished in the table?

(a) 11th   (b) 13th   (c) 15th

12 How many players did Wolves use during the season – in league games only?

(a) 30   (b) 32   (c) 34

13 Sylvan Ebanks-Blake was Wolves' most-used substitute – how many times did he come off the bench in all competitions?

(a) 17   (b) 21   (c) 25

14 How many different Wolves players found the net in the league during the season?

(a) 14   (b) 15   (c) 16

15 How many shots on target did Wolves muster in the Barclays Premier League in the 2010/11 season?

(a) 158   (b) 208   (c) 258

Answers on page 61!

Matt Jarvis

49

we can be HEROES

The Wolves players may be heroes to many fans – but who did the players themselves look up to in their formative years?

We asked a selection for their sporting heroes whom they followed keenly while growing up.

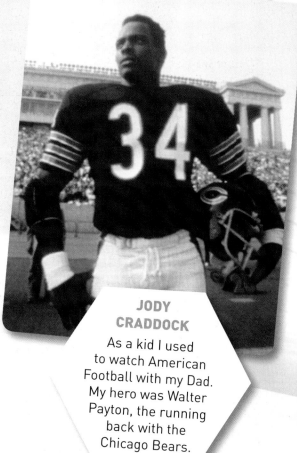

WAYNE HENNESSEY

Mine would have to be Neville Southall. As an up-and-coming goalkeeper I loved watching him play for Wales and was fortunate enough to be coached by him in the international set-up.

JODY CRADDOCK

As a kid I used to watch American Football with my Dad. My hero was Walter Payton, the running back with the Chicago Bears.

ADLENE GUEDIOURA

Roberto Baggio was a great footballer I used to watch when I was growing up. Also Mohammed Ali for what he was like outside the ring. What a personality!

KEVIN FOLEY

For me it would be Eric Cantona. Watching him play he always had that something about him. He was untouchable!

MICHAEL KIGHTLY

Ryan Giggs. For me as a young winger he was so exciting to watch and it's great to see he is still going strong all these years later.

STEPHEN WARD

I was a Manchester United fan as a kid and so it would have to be Ryan Giggs. An absolute legend.

MATT JARVIS

My idol was always Ryan Giggs when I was growing up. He was just lightning quick, running around everyone and scoring goals and it's amazing he's still going so well now.

CARL IKEME

I loved to watch Mike Tyson fight – he was an animal!

RONALD ZUBAR

It would be Andre Agassi for me. I quite like watching tennis and as a kid watching Agassi was always very exciting.

CHRISTOPHE BERRA

My hero as a kid would be Marcel Desailly. Obviously he is one of the best central defenders there has been and with my Dad being French he was the perfect choice.

SYLVAN EBANKS-BLAKE

I admired Andy Cole as a kid when he was at Manchester United. He's a real goalscorer and the sort of goals he scores are the ones I like to score.

RICHARD STEARMAN

This one will probably get me some stick but it would be Steve Walsh from Leicester! Having moved to Leicester I followed the team and he was the player I had as my hero.

STEPHEN HUNT

Faustino Asprilla. He was both flamboyant and unpredictable, and it was exciting watching him not really knowing what he was going to do next.

KARL HENRY

I used to love watching Alan Shearer as a kid, particularly when he was playing and scoring so many goals for Blackburn. He was a great striker.

JAMIE O'HARA

For me it would have to be Paul Gascoigne. He's just a legend isn't he? The way he played the game was just great to watch. And Paul Scholes was another player I really admired as well.

KEVIN DOYLE

I wouldn't say one particular hero, but any one of that Republic of Ireland team from the World Cup in 1990. I watched it all on television and it was great to see them go all the way to the quarter finals.

TEN THINGS you never knew about KARL HENRY

Karl Henry, born and bred in Wolverhampton, has taken great pride in his role in the club's successes over the last five years, much of which he spent as club captain.

The midfielder was one of Mick McCarthy's first signings when he took over in the summer of 2006 and had chalked up 198 appearances in all competitions by the end of the 2010/11 campaign.

Always a major influence both on and off the pitch, Henry has been a figurehead for much of the progress Wolves have made in the years under McCarthy.

The Wolves Annual caught up to delve a little deeper into the background of King Henry – and to find out a few things which people may not know about the Wolves number 8.

Over to Karl...

The great debaters! Henry and Jones.

Picture: Denise Winter Photography

Mr and Mrs Henry.

1 I'm a Chess Master! My Dad taught me and my sister how to play chess when we were kids. I started playing again more recently with Bill Stevens the club's Sports Therapist and have been wiping the floor with him. The Club Doctor Matt Perry has been wiping the floor with both of us. I play Chess Jam online as well. I'm sounding like a bit of a geek now. But I've got a decent win/loss ratio.

2 I got married to Lucy in the summer. We met in Cyprus on holiday nine years ago. Lucy's employed as a fundraiser and works at a school in Birmingham.

3 I went to Coppice High School and we represented Wolverhampton at Year 9 (Under-14s) in getting to Wembley. We played on the pitch at Wembley before the Crystal Palace/Leicester play-off final of 1996. We were up against a team representing Millwall but lost on penalties. I didn't take one. It was sudden death straightaway and we had another star player called Ben Rix who took the first penalty and missed it. They took

Skipper's musical choice
– Luciano Pavarotti

theirs and scored. I had a goal disallowed in the game – for being in the area!

4 I like all sorts of music and am listening to a bit more classical stuff as I get older and more mature. I love 'Time to Say Goodbye' by Andrea Bocelli. My Mum also gave me an album – 'Pavarotti Love Songs'. There's a song on there called 'Il Canto' which I really like. In my car I mainly listen to Hip Hop and R&B as well as Indie music like Oasis, I also like the big vocals like Frank Sinatra and Tony Bennett. I play an acoustic guitar after being taught by my friend when I was younger and have carried on teaching myself. I am also teaching myself to play the piano and keyboard.

5 My best friends in football are probably Darel Russell (Preston), Kris Commons (Celtic) and Lewis Buxton (Sheffield Wednesday). They were all best men at my wedding along with another friend from school – a policeman called Simon Davies. Had I known David Jones a bit longer he'd probably have been my fifth best man because we get on really well.

6 I have more debates with David Jones than anybody else, on all sorts of topics. The biggest debate we have is a religious one which goes on daily. He's religious and I'm an agnostic, or unsure. Jonah is trying to sway me, so we have a lot of debates and discussions on that.

Karl lining up for Bushbury Boys
(back row, fourth from right).

7 When I was a kid I played all the usual other sports, tennis, cricket – although that wasn't for me – and I've done a bit of golf, snooker and pool. I'm a pool shark actually and will take on anyone that fancies it. Bring it on. I fancy myself against anybody, and I mean anybody. I actually entered the leagues at Riley's in Wolverhampton – but I never turned up! My friend was involved so I put my name down, but then he quit and as he was my link man I had to pull out. I was down there in the fixtures but it never happened. Maybe one day.

8 I was a wheeler-dealer at school. I used to buy those Micro Chips, four packs for a pound. I'd go home at break time, put them all in the microwave and then go back and sell them all

Ben Foster the perennial winner.

for a pound each. 300 per cent profit! I only lived two doors away from the school so when we had a ten minute break after the first two lessons I'd run home and do that.

9 I stayed in digs at Stoke. When we used to play darts, snooker and pool and all that stuff I was the top man at everything. At least I was until Ben Foster came in. He was a little bit better than me at everything. And that hurt me, as anyone that knows me will realise!

10 My first ever team was Bushbury Boys at the age of nine or ten. My first game was in the rain, for the age group above. I remember my step dad standing on the sidelines shouting at me to get stuck in for the whole game. It was raining, I had my sleeves down, and it wasn't much fun!

WOLVES AID
helping the community

Wolves Aid is the fundraising arm of the club's charity – Wolves Community Trust – and has been donating to good causes in the local community since 1993.

Since April 2008, Wolves Aid has been able to donate even more money after Wolves' chairman Steve Morgan started to hand over a proportion of The Morgan Foundation's budget to the charity.

Wolves Aid specialises in supporting small to medium sized locally based organisations whose work focuses on children, families, disadvantage and disability. Any work which has a positive effect on the welfare and quality of life, or which enhances the opportunities and life choices for people in and around the Wolverhampton area will be considered.

Approximately £323,000 had been donated by Wolves Aid between April 2008 and June 2011, and much more since. Visit the Wolves Aid section at **www.wolvescommunitytrust.org** for details.

In the meantime here are a few of the causes which have been supported:

A donation from Wolves Aid helped with a fundraising drive to refurbish the Wolverhampton branch of the Samaritans. Improvements included new disabled access and a new training room for face-to-face sessions.

Wayne Hennessey and Dave Edwards popped into the Albrighton Moat Project, a day centre supported by Wolves Aid which provides disabled people of all ages with motivational activities.

Matt Murray and Wolfie visited Green Park School, a special school for pupils with severe learning difficulties. Wolves Aid has provided specialist playground equipment for the school, where pupils arrive to the strains of 'Hi Ho Silver Lining' every morning!

CEO Jez Moxey presented a cheque to the Westcroft Community Foundation, the charitable arm of Westcroft School and Sports College. Westcroft is a special school which provides sporting activities – including sailing – to disabled pupils and other youngsters from the local community, and were in need of new equipment.

And finally... Steve Morgan also donned his running shoes this year as part of the Morgan Foundation's work for Water Aid in Rwanda. Steve and colleague Dave Edwards completed the London Marathon and, with the Wolves Chairman matching all donations received, raised an incredible £87,000 for the campaign to bring clean water to a community in the poverty-hit country.

ROGER AND IN!

Mick McCarthy and Roger Johnson had spoken long before Wolves' summer signing arrived at Molineux for talks over his move from Birmingham City.

It was in May to be precise, when the Wolves manager and his future captain had a slight disagreement about whether a ball was being returned into play quickly enough in the game at St Andrew's.

"We exchanged a few pleasantries didn't we Rog?" said McCarthy at the press conference to announce Johnson's arrival.

"He thought I was trying to hang onto the ball but in reality I was trying to give it him back."

"Was he right Roger?" came a reporter's question.

"Maybe…"

But it was that brief exchange which told McCarthy more than he ever needed to know about the centre half he had been pursuing for over two years.

"I want commanding players – players who demand things of themselves and their team-mates and are vocal out on the pitch," says McCarthy.

"Whatever I liked about him before I liked even more after that exchange at St Andrew's when he 'had it' with me – 'fair do's, I thought at the time!"

Johnson is a defender who prefers that personality to shine through on the pitch rather than in talking about his qualities off it.

But he certainly checked in at Molineux keen to prove his worth and continue the excellent form shown with Birmingham, which saw him land a Carling Cup winner's medal thanks to February's win against Arsenal.

"I've been lucky with managers in that they've been a bit like myself," he said.

If there's something to be said I'll say it and I'm sure the gaffer is pretty much the same.

That's a major thing, there are no hiding places, nothing is left unsaid and that's the way it should be.

I'm really pleased to have joined Wolves and there were a lot of things which attracted me to the club.

I know a few of the boys already, it means I can stay in the area, but more than that I think Wolves are a club who are really going places at the moment."

DOYLER'S TOP10

Kevin Doyle has been a key performer for Wolves since arriving as the club's then record signing in the summer of 2009.

The popular Irish striker has won plenty of admirers for his selfless approach and performances as Wolves clinched back-to-back survivals in the Barclays Premier League.

He has also been among the goals, as he has throughout his career.

The Wolves Annual caught up with Kevin ahead of the 2011/12 season to find out his favourite goals so far, based not only on the quality of the goals but also their significance.

So, in chronological order, here – drum roll please – is Doyler's top ten.

Doyle's duck broken for the Republic of Ireland against San Marino.

FIRST GOAL FOR READING (29/08/05)

My first goal for Reading came against Burnley and it proved to be a winner. It was a header from a cross from Bobby Convey with about 20 minutes left.

PROMOTION CLINCHER (25/03/06)

Another header this one, after a corner was flicked on in our game at Leicester. I think a certain Richard Stearman was playing for the opposition – he was probably supposed to be marking me! We drew the game 1-1 which secured promotion to the Premier League.

FIRST GOAL FOR IRELAND (15/11/06)

My first goal for Ireland came in a qualifier for Euro 2008 and was the last game played at Lansdowne Road. We beat San Marino 5-0 and my header to Kevin Kilbane's cross went in off the bar.

FIRST IN THE PREMIER LEAGUE (23/08/06)

My first in the Premier League came for Reading at Aston Villa. There were only a few minutes gone and I headed home a cross from Seol Ki-Hyeon. I then celebrated by sliding on my knees in front of the Holte End – not the cleverest thing I've ever done!

A first Premier League goal at Villa – in front of the Holte End!

Perfect flicked header earns the points at Tottenham.

FIRST AGAINST UNITED (23/09/06)

It may have been a penalty but I was delighted to score against Manchester United as I'd supported them as a kid. It would have been a winner but Ronaldo equalised in the second half. I managed to get another for Wolves against United last season despite George (Elokobi) trying to grab it off me!

FAVOURITE FOR IRELAND (08/09/07)

One of my favourite goals for Ireland came in an away game at Slovakia. It was a shot on the turn with my left foot and one I particularly enjoyed.

FIRST FOR WOLVES (20/09/09)

A first goal for your new club is always special and I was pleased to get off the mark against Fulham. I think Christophe (Berra) flicked on a throw and I managed to get in to score with a header before celebrating with the crowd.

EARNING HIS SPURS (12/12/09)

My header against Spurs at White Hart Lane was a fairly simple one, from Nenad's free kick. But it proved important as we hung on for a 1-0 win which was a really big result against one of the league's bigger teams.

Slides the ball inside the post against West Ham.

HAMMER BLOW (23/03/10)

I managed to seize on a mistake from a defender to run in and score with a low shot against West Ham. It was such a big night for us at the end of a massive ten days in the season, and after the goal we managed to go on and win 3-1.

ANDORRA (06/09/10)

Another for Ireland, and another with my left foot. I managed to catch it really well from the edge of the area and it flew into the top corner.

Celebrating with the Wolves fans after first goal for the club against Fulham.

STAND and DELIVER

As soon as Wolves' clinched their Barclays Premier League survival on the final day of the 2010/11 season, it was time to head straight into the next exciting phase of the club's future with the redevelopment of Molineux.

A key ambition of Wolves' owner and chairman Steve Morgan, the board pressed the button on redevelopment earlier in the year, ensuring preparatory work could be carried out on the first phase of the redevelopment – the Stan Cullis Stand – prior to it being demolished once the season was over.

Contractors The Buckingham Group quickly set about changing the face of the stand with a seamless demolition before laying the foundations for the new structure to rise from the ground.

Supporters also took a keen interest via a live webcam set up which could be viewed at the special redevelopment website – www.molineuxpride.co.uk

Below are a few photographs taken of the redevelopment work which took place over the summer, alongside images of what the stand will look like when completed ahead of the start of the 2012/13 campaign.

Fans are asked to note that the final Computer Generated Images are an indication only and may be subject to slight change in the final process.

a kit of all right!

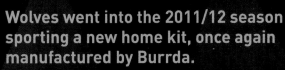

Wolves went into the 2011/12 season sporting a new home kit, once again manufactured by Burrda.

The kit was first unveiled at the club's end of season dinner, as shown in the picture to the right with 'models' for the night George Elokobi, Matt Jarvis and Adlene Guedioura.

Local specialist photographic company SM2 Studio were also drafted in to work their magic with some publicity pictures, as illustrated above with several of the first team squad 'transported' to the height of Wolverhampton looking over the city centre below.

Then of course the shirt went on sale, with Wolves fan Jay Philpot one of the first into the club's Molineux retail store to pick one up.

Quiz Answers

```
S T A N C U L L I S R E W O L F N O R J
O Y X O U L E S S T E V E B U R P E O E
B I L L L J E A Y A L E X R E A S N B L
E I M V P O B I L L Y W R I G H T A B L
R O I K A H J D O J O H A O N C E E I E
T D C E N N R O O B D S E J B H V K E W
W A K N E R C D I L N H T L I B E E D N
I V M N L I Y B I K I H C A R C B I E R
L P C Y L C T A A Q V S N T N T U B N A
L M C H U H M A T N E I E I U U L B N B
I A I M A B J A C K W F N L M L O I N
A L R B Y R E O O R S S M D O U Y R S H
M C T B M D T A A D T C B C L J A D O O
S E H I M S R P R P A U L L N C E P N J
T I Y T I T K O Y X N D I L A B N V N A
E D L T J E S S E E B D A V K S E A R
V D A V R E T A L S L L I B R L E Y O D
D E R E K D O U G A N P A U L I N C E E
J O D Y C R A D D O C K E Y P E S S E J
Z G H Y E L K C U B K N A R F R O J A M
```

THE NUMBERS GAME (page 48)

1. (a) Newcastle
2. (a) 15
3. (c) Blackpool
4. (b) Matt Jarvis
5. (b) 13th
6. (a) 10
7. (b) 30
8. (b) 12
9. (c) 5
10. (a) Stephen Ward
11. (a) 11th
12. (a) 30
13. (b) 21
14. (c) 16
15. (b) 208

WHO SAID IT? (page 30)

1. Karl Henry
2. Ronald Zubar
3. Kevin Doyle
4. Robert Plant
5. Steve Morgan
6. Matt Jarvis
7. Michael Kightly
8. Marcus Hahnemann (APRIL FOOL!)
9. Stephen Hunt
10. Mick McCarthy

Where's Wolfie!